The Rise and Fall of Empires:

A Journey Through the Course of Human History

BY

Jason K. Pettry

Copyright © 2023 by Jason K. Pettry

The Rise and Fall of Empires: A Journey Through the Course of Human History

TABLE OF CONTENT

INTRODUCTION

Once upon a time, an ancient kingdom rose to great power and glory. Its people were brave and its cities were bustling with life. But, as all empires do, it eventually fell. From the ashes of the old kingdom, a new one arose. This nation was strong and proud and its people had a newfound sense of purpose and ambition. But, as all empires do, it too eventually fell.

This cycle of rise and fall repeated itself throughout human history. Empires would come and go, with each one leaving its unique legacy. Some of these empires were short-lived, while others lasted for centuries. Some were strong, while others were weak and vulnerable.

But the journey of these empires was always the same. They would rise and conquer, then eventually fall and be forgotten. The rise and fall of empires was a journey that would continue throughout human history, each new empire leaving its mark on the world.

From the great Persian Empire to the mighty Roman Empire, from the British Empire to the Chinese dynasties, each of these empires has left its unique legacy on the world. They have shaped the course of human history, and they will continue to do so in the future. So take a journey through the rise and fall of empires: a journey through the course of human history. Discover the stories of the great empires that have come and gone, and learn how they have shaped our world today.

The rise and fall of empires: a journey through the course of human history.

Throughout history, the rise and fall of empires have been a constant theme. From the ancient empires of Mesopotamia, Egypt, and China, to the medieval empires of Byzantium, the Islamic Caliphate, and the Mongols, to the early modern empires of Spain, Portugal, and Britain, to the modern empires of America, Russia, and Japan, empires have shaped the course of human history in profound ways.

Empires have brought civilization, order, and prosperity to some while causing suffering, destruction, and exploitation to others. They have expanded borders, spread cultures, and imposed languages, religions, and values on diverse peoples. They have invented systems of government, law, and administration, and left behind great works of art, literature, and science. They have also triggered wars, rebellions, and revolutions, and provoked resistance, nationalism, and anti-imperialism.

To understand empires is to understand human nature, human societies, and human destiny. It is to confront the paradox of power and its limits, the dialectic of unity and diversity, and the challenge of balance and justice. It is to learn from the mistakes and achievements of the past and to reflect on the choices and dilemmas of the present and future.

This book aims to provide a comprehensive and insightful overview of the history of empires, from the earliest civilizations to the present day. It will explore the origins, growth, and decline of empires, the factors that enabled or hindered their success, and the legacies they left behind. It will also analyze the debates and controversies surrounding empires, from their justification and impact to their morality and ethics.

By embarking on this journey through the course of human history, we hope to gain a deeper understanding of who we are, where we came from, and where we are going. Join us on this adventure into the world of empires.

DEFINING EMPIRES.

Defining Empires is a complex task that has been debated by historians, philosophers, and political scientists for centuries. Generally, an empire can be defined as a political entity that exercises power and control over a group of territories, peoples, and resources beyond its borders, usually through military conquest, colonization, or diplomacy.

However, this definition does not capture the full range and diversity of empires throughout history. Empires have varied in size, duration, ideology, and structure, and have included different types of polities, such as city-states, kingdoms, republics, caliphates, and federations. Moreover, empires have had different motivations and objectives, such as economic gain, ideological hegemony, security, prestige, or humanitarianism. Some scholars argue that empires are characterized by a distinct pattern of expansion, centralization, and domination, in which the imperial center imposes its rule on the periphery, often by force or coercion, and extracts resources and tribute from the subjugated regions. Empires also tend to promote a sense of identity, loyalty, and hierarchy among their subjects, often through the dissemination of a common language, culture, religion, or ideology.

Other scholars question the legitimacy and morality of empires, arguing that they involve the violation of human rights, sovereignty, and dignity, and contribute to inequality, conflict, and oppression. They also point out the contradictions and inconsistencies of imperial ideology, which often claims to promote freedom, justice, and civilization, while perpetuating violence, exploitation, and cultural destruction.

Empires are defined as large, complex political entity that controls multiple nations, regions, and/or people. Empires were first formed in ancient times and have continued to exist throughout history. Empires are often characterized by an expansive territory, centralized power, and a hierarchical structure of rulers and subjects. Empires have also been known to encompass a variety of cultures, languages, and religions. The most successful empires have been those that have successfully maintained their power through military force, economic prosperity, and effective government. Empires are not only fascinating to study but can provide important lessons about the development of human societies.

Throughout history, many empires have come and gone, leaving behind a legacy of greatness and power. Empires such as the Roman Empire, the Persian Empire, and the British Empire are all examples of the various types of empires that have existed throughout time. Each of these empires had unique characteristics, and each was influential in its way. Empires are often studied to gain a greater understanding of how civilizations develop, how different societies interact, and how power and authority are maintained.

The legacy of empires continues to be felt in our world today. Empires have helped shape the modern political landscape, as well as our understanding of the world. Empires continue to influence our understanding of what it means to be a nation, the importance of culture and language, and the power of the state. As such, studying the history and development of empires is an important part of understanding the world around us.

Empires are fascinating to study and can provide a great deal of insight into the world around us. Empires give us a unique perspective on how societies develop, the power dynamics between nations, and the consequences of imperial rule. Empires are an important part of understanding the world around us, and studying them can help us gain a greater appreciation of the past, as well as a better understanding of the present.

Empires are an important part of history and continue to shape our lives today. By studying empires, we can gain a greater understanding of the world around us. Empires provide us with an important perspective on how societies develop, how power is maintained, and how different cultures interact. Empires are a fascinating topic to study and can provide a great deal of insight into the past and present.

In summary, defining empires requires a nuanced and contextualized approach that takes into account the diverse historical, cultural, and political factors that shape them.

Empires can be seen as both a source of innovation, integration, and diversity, and a source of conflict, domination, and exploitation. Understanding the nature and impact of empires is crucial for understanding the dynamics of world history and the challenges of global governance and cooperation today.

WHY STUDY EMPIRES?

Studying empires is an important and fascinating way to understand the history of the world. Empires were the major forces of political, social, cultural, and economic change throughout history. By studying empires, we can learn about the origins of globalization, the development of different political systems, the spread of religion and culture, and the interaction between different cultures. We can also gain insights into the development of different economic systems, the growth of international trade, the rise of global communication, and the formation of distinct identities. Empires have shaped the world as we know it, and by studying them we can better understand our own current global political and economic circumstances. Studying empires also allows us to explore the motivations behind the imperial expansion, the ethical and legal implications of imperialism, and the consequences of imperialism on indigenous populations. By examining the successes and failures of different empires, we can gain a better understanding of the complexities of international relations. Finally, studying empires can help us to develop an appreciation of the diversity of human cultures and societies, and to gain a better understanding of our place in the world.

In short, studying empires is essential to gaining a nuanced understanding of the past and present, and to developing a deeper appreciation of our place in the world.

Why Studying Empires is a question that has intrigued scholars and the public alike for centuries. The answer lies in the fact that empires have played a crucial role in shaping human history, culture, and society. Here are some compelling reasons why studying empires is essential:

Understanding Power and Politics: Empires are an excellent case study for understanding how power and politics operate on a global scale. Studying empires allows us to understand how emperors, kings, and rulers wielded power and how they maintained their dominance over vast territories and diverse peoples. It also helps us to comprehend how these empires influenced global power structures and geopolitical relations.

Analyzing Societal Transformations: Empires have not only been important political entities but also have brought about significant societal changes. By studying empires, we can gain insight into how societies have evolved and how cultures have interacted with each other. Empires have facilitated trade, migration, and cultural exchange, leading to the emergence of new ideas, customs, and technologies.

Examining Ethics and Morality: Empires raise important ethical and moral questions. The rise and fall of empires have often been accompanied by violence, oppression, and exploitation of weaker groups. The study of empires can help us to reflect on the morality of imperialism and its impact on subjugated populations.

Exploring Art, Literature, and Science: Empires have often been centers of creativity and innovation. The study of empires allows us to explore the rich cultural legacy of these civilizations, from literature and art to philosophy and science.

Learning from History: Studying empires provides valuable lessons for understanding current global affairs. By examining the successes and failures of past empires, we can gain insights into the challenges of global governance and cooperation today. In conclusion, studying empires is essential for understanding human history and society, politics, and power, ethics and morality, art and culture, and learning from history. Empires have played a crucial role in shaping the world as we know it, and by studying them, we can better understand the complex and dynamic nature of global interactions.

OVERVIEW OF THE BOOK

Explore the fascinating journey of human history and uncover the rise and fall of empires, from the earliest civilizations to the modern day. In The Rise and Fall of Empires, author Jason K. Pettry takes readers on an enlightening journey through the ages, exploring how civilizations have grown, changed, and ultimately declined. Follow the stories of famous leaders and rulers who have shaped the course of history and discover the powerful forces which have determined the fate of empires. Along the way, uncover the strategies and tactics employed by leaders to stay in power and gain insight into the complex relationship between political, economic, and social forces. Immerse yourself in a captivating journey through the past and gain valuable insights into the course of human history.

The Rise and Fall of Empires is an essential read for anyone interested in learning about the many empires that have shaped history.

"The Rise and Fall of Empires: A Journey Through the Course of Human History" is a captivating exploration of the rise and fall of empires throughout the ages. From the ancient empires of Greece and Rome to the mighty empires of the British and Ottoman, this book takes the reader on a journey through the complex and dynamic world of imperial power.

With a comprehensive and engaging approach, this book examines the political, economic, social, and cultural factors that shaped empires and their legacies. It provides an in-depth analysis of the rise and fall of empires, their impact on the world, and the challenges of global governance and cooperation today.

Drawing on the latest research and scholarship, this book offers a unique perspective on world history and provides valuable insights into the complexities and contradictions of empires. It challenges readers to reflect on the nature and impact of imperialism, its legacies, and the ethical and moral questions it raises.

Whether you are a student of history, politics, or international relations, or simply a curious reader, "The Rise and Fall of Empires" is a must-read. It is a journey through the course of human history that is both fascinating and enlightening and will leave you with a deeper understanding of the world we live in today.

PART I: ANCIENT EMPIRES
MESOPOTAMIA: THE CRADLE OF CIVILIZATION

Mesopotamia is an area of the Middle East that is often referred to as the "cradle of civilization." This region is considered to be the birthplace of many of the world's earliest civilizations and was home to the ancient Sumerians, Babylonians, and Assyrians. Mesopotamia is located in the area currently known as Iraq and parts of Turkey, Iran, and Syria.

Mesopotamia is known for its rich history and culture and is credited with many technological and social advances of the ancient world. It is believed to be the birthplace of written language, agriculture, and irrigation. Mesopotamian societies were also highly organized, with a complex legal system and a strong governance structure.

The area was also home to several important religious traditions, including the worship of many gods, such as Anu, Enlil, Enki, and Inanna. Temples, or ziggurats, were built to honor these gods and were often the center of religious and political life.

Mesopotamia is an incredibly important area of the world and has played a major role in the development of many aspects of modern life. Its influence can be seen in many aspects of our current culture and society, from language and writing.

Today, the area is home to many archaeological sites and remains of ancient cities, which are now popular tourist attractions. It is rich history and cultural significance continue to make Mesopotamia an important destination for tourists and scholars alike.

Mesopotamia, also known as the "land between two rivers," is widely recognized as the cradle of civilization

The Mesopotamian civilization emerged around 4000 BCE, with the development of agriculture and the domestication of animals. This allowed for the growth of cities and the emergence of complex societies. The fertile land between the Tigris and Euphrates rivers provided an abundant food supply and supported the development of a sophisticated irrigation system. The Mesopotamians were known for their technological innovations, such as the invention of the wheel, the plow, and writing. They also developed a complex system of laws, codes, and institutions that influenced later civilizations, such as the Babylonian Code of Hammurabi.

Religion played a significant role in Mesopotamian society, with polytheistic beliefs and the worship of numerous gods and goddesses. The Mesopotamians built impressive temples and ziggurats, which served as centers of religious and political power.

Despite its many achievements, the Mesopotamian civilization faced numerous challenges, such as warfare, invasion, and environmental disasters. The region was repeatedly conquered by various empires, including the Persians, Greeks, and Romans. Today, the legacy of Mesopotamia can be seen in modern-day Iraq and the wider Middle East. Its contributions to civilization, such as writing, law, and agriculture, continue to influence the world today. Mesopotamia remains an important part of human history and a testament to the ingenuity and resilience of early human civilizations.

THE FALL OF MESOPOTAMIA

The fall of Mesopotamia can be attributed to a combination of factors, including invasion, internal conflict, and environmental disasters.

One of the major factors that contributed to the fall of Mesopotamia was invasion. The region was conquered by various empires throughout its history, including the Persians, Greeks, and Romans. These invasions often led to the destruction of cities and the displacement of populations.

Internal conflict was another factor that contributed to the fall of Mesopotamia. The region was marked by frequent warfare between city-states and empires, which weakened its political and social structures. This internal conflict made Mesopotamia vulnerable to external invasion and conquest.

Environmental disasters, such as drought and flooding, also played a role in the decline of Mesopotamia. The region was heavily dependent on irrigation for agriculture, and when the irrigation systems failed, crops failed, and famine ensued. This led to social unrest and further weakened the region's ability to defend itself.

The fall of Mesopotamia was a gradual process that spanned several centuries. By the 7th century CE, the region was conquered by the Arab Muslim armies, and Islam became the dominant religion. The Arab conquest marked the end of the ancient Mesopotamian civilization and the beginning of a new era in the region's history.

Despite the fall of the ancient Mesopotamian civilization, its legacy lives on in modern-day Iraq and the wider Middle East. The region's contributions to civilization, such as writing, law, and agriculture, continue to influence the world today. Mesopotamia remains an important part of human history and a testament to the ingenuity and resilience of early human civilizations.

EGYPT: THE LAND OF PHARAOHS

Egypt is an ancient country located in the northeastern corner of Africa. It is known as the Land of Pharaohs due to its long and illustrious history.

The history of Egypt is as old as civilization itself. It is the birthplace of some of the world's earliest civilizations, including the Ancient Egyptians and their powerful Pharaohs.

The Ancient Egyptians built grand monuments, complex irrigation systems and impressive papyrus documents. They also developed mathematics, astronomy and hieroglyphic writing.

The Ancient Egyptians were also renowned for their mummification practices, which were used to preserve the bodies of the deceased.

Today, Egypt is home to the Pyramids of Giza, the Great Sphinx and the Valley of the Kings. These ancient monuments are a testament to the greatness of the Ancient Egyptians and their powerful Pharaohs.

Egypt is also known for its cultural diversity, with a mix of Arab, African and Mediterranean influences. Visitors to Egypt can explore the country's many historical sites, enjoy its stunning beaches, visit its vibrant markets and take part in its rich cultural activities.

Egypt is a country filled with adventure and mystery. From the Great Pyramids to the tombs of the Pharaohs, Egypt is a land rich in history and culture. Visitors can explore its monuments, taste its delicious cuisine, shop in its bustling bazaars and take part in its vibrant nightlife.

No matter how you choose to experience it, Egypt is a country that will leave you with an unforgettable experience.

It has a rich history, dating back to ancient times when it was ruled by powerful dynasties of pharaohs, who built magnificent pyramids and temples that still stand today. Egypt has also played a significant role in shaping world civilization, from its contributions to art, science, and literature to its influence on religion and politics.

One of the most iconic features of Egypt is its ancient monuments. The pyramids of Giza, one of the Seven Wonders of the World, are the most recognizable symbols of Egypt. Built over 4,500 years ago, these massive structures were tombs for pharaohs and their consorts, filled with treasures and artifacts that provide insight into the lives and beliefs of the ancient Egyptians. Other notable monuments include the Sphinx, the temples of Luxor and Karnak, and the Valley of the Kings, where the pharaohs were buried.

Aside from its ancient history, Egypt is also a country of diverse landscapes and cultures. The Nile River, which flows through the country from south to north, has sustained Egypt's people and agriculture for millennia. The Nile Delta, where the river empties into the Mediterranean Sea, is a fertile area known for its agriculture and fishing. The Sahara Desert covers most of the country, but there are also oases and mountain ranges that provide a haven for wildlife and humans alike.

Egypt's culture is a blend of ancient and modern influences. Egyptian music, dance, and literature have a long and rich history, but the country has also embraced contemporary art forms and media. Islam is the dominant religion in Egypt, and the Islamic influence is visible in the architecture, art, and customs of the country. However, Egypt is also home to a significant Christian minority, as well as small Jewish and Bahá'í communities.

Egypt's political history has been turbulent in recent decades, with periods of unrest and revolution. However, the country remains a vital player in the Middle East and North Africa region, with a strategic location and a strong economy based on tourism, agriculture, and industry. The people of Egypt are known for their hospitality, warmth, and love of life, and visitors to the country are often struck by the beauty and richness of its culture and history.

In conclusion, Egypt is a country that has captured the imagination of people around the world for centuries. With its ancient monuments, diverse landscapes, and vibrant culture, it is a place that offers something for everyone. Whether you are interested in history, art, religion, or simply want to experience a different way of life, Egypt is a destination that should be on every traveler's bucket list.

Egyptian civilization has been around for more than 5,000 years and is one of the oldest and most enduring in human history. During this time, Egypt has seen the rise and fall of many powerful empires, including the Old Kingdom, Middle Kingdom, and New Kingdom, which are often referred to as the "Empire of the Pharaohs."

The Old Kingdom, which lasted from around 2686 BC to 2181 BC, was the first of the great Egyptian empires. It was during this time that the pharaohs began to build the great pyramids of Giza, which are some of the most famous and enduring monuments of ancient Egypt. The pharaohs of the Old Kingdom were also responsible for developing a complex system of government and administration, which helped to create a stable and prosperous society.

The Middle Kingdom, which lasted from around 2055 BC to 1650 BC, was a time of great cultural and artistic achievement in Egypt. The pharaohs of the Middle Kingdom built many impressive temples and tombs, including the temple of Karnak and the tombs of the Valley of the Kings. They also developed a strong navy, which helped to expand Egypt's influence and trade throughout the Mediterranean region.

The New Kingdom, which lasted from around 1550 BC to 1070 BC, was the most powerful and prosperous period in Egyptian history. It was during this time that Egypt reached the height of its military and economic power, conquering neighboring lands and establishing an empire that stretched from Nubia in the south to Syria in the north. The pharaohs of the New Kingdom were also responsible for building many of the most impressive temples and monuments in Egypt, including the temple of Abu Simbel and the mortuary temple of Hatshepsut.

Throughout these various empires, the pharaohs of Egypt were seen as both divine rulers and earthly kings. They were believed to be responsible for maintaining the order and balance of the universe, and their power and influence extended into all aspects of Egyptian society. The pharaohs were also known for their wealth and extravagance, and many of the great monuments and temples of Egypt were built to honor them and their accomplishments.

Despite the decline of the pharaonic dynasties and the many changes that Egypt has undergone over the centuries, the legacy of the Empire of the Pharaohs lives on in the country's rich cultural heritage and enduring monuments. Today, Egypt remains one of the most fascinating and awe-inspiring places in the world, a testament to the enduring power and influence of one of the greatest empires in human history.

CHINA: FROM XIA TO HAN

China is one of the oldest civilizations in the world, with a history that stretches back over 4,000 years. The earliest known Chinese dynasties were the Xia, Shang, and Zhou dynasties, which were all located in the Yellow River Valley.

The Xia Dynasty (c. 2100-1600 BCE) was the first known dynasty in China, though it is possible there were earlier dynasties that have not been recorded in history. During the Xia Dynasty, the Chinese people developed a writing system and began to use bronze tools. They also began to build large cities and developed a legal system.

The Shang Dynasty (c. 1600-1046 BCE) followed the Xia Dynasty and is considered the first true Chinese dynasty. During the Shang Dynasty, the Chinese people developed a system of writing, developed strong religious beliefs, and built large cities.

The Zhou Dynasty (c. 1046-256 BCE) followed the Shang Dynasty and is considered the longest-lasting dynasty in Chinese history. During the Zhou Dynasty, the Chinese people developed a system of philosophy and established a strong central government. They also developed a system of writing, standardized weights and measures, and built large cities.

The Han Dynasty (206 BCE-220 CE) followed the Zhou Dynasty and is considered one of the most influential dynasties in Chinese history. During the Han Dynasty, the Chinese people developed a strong civil service system, built the Great Wall of China, and established Confucianism as the official state philosophy. They also developed a system of writing, standardized weights and measures, and built large cities.

From the Xia to the Han Dynasty, China experienced a period of incredible growth and development. The Chinese people established a strong central government, developed a system of writing, and built large cities. They also established

Confucianism as their official state philosophy and developed a strong civil service system. Through these accomplishments, the Chinese people laid the foundation for the modern Chinese state. The Xia dynasty is considered the first dynasty of China, and although there is little concrete evidence to support its existence, it is believed to have laid the foundation for many of the institutions and traditions that would become hallmarks of Chinese culture. It was during the Xia dynasty that the Chinese first developed a system of writing, created a calendar based on the phases of the moon, and established a system of government and law.

The Shang dynasty, which followed the Xia, was the first dynasty for which there is significant archaeological evidence. It was during the Shang dynasty that the Chinese first began to use bronze to make tools, weapons, and ritual vessels, and the art and craftsmanship of this period are considered some of the finest in Chinese history. The Shang dynasty also saw the development of a sophisticated system of divination and oracle bones, which were used to predict the future and communicate with the gods.

The Zhou dynasty, which followed the Shang, was one of the longest-lasting and most influential dynasties in Chinese history. It was during the Zhou dynasty that Confucianism, Taoism, and other philosophical and religious traditions began to emerge, and the influence of these traditions would continue to shape Chinese culture for centuries to come. The Zhou dynasty was also marked by significant technological advancements, including the invention of iron tools and weapons and the development of a system of roads and canals that helped to facilitate trade and commerce.

The Han dynasty, which followed the Qin dynasty, was a time of great expansion and consolidation in China. It was during the Han dynasty that the Chinese first began to use paper, which revolutionized communication and record-keeping, and it was also during this period that the Great Wall of China was built to protect the empire from foreign invaders. The Han dynasty was also known for its advancements in science and technology, including the invention of the seismograph and the water clock, and its contributions to art, literature, and philosophy.

Throughout China's long and complex history, there have been numerous empires and dynasties that have shaped the country's culture, politics, and society. From the legendary Xia dynasty to the powerful Han dynasty, China's past is marked by a rich and diverse array of traditions, innovations, and achievements that continue to influence the world today.

GREECE: BIRTHPLACE OF DEMOCRACY

Greece is widely known as the birthplace of democracy. The ancient Greeks developed the first known democratic system of government over 2,500 years ago. This system of government emphasized equality and the rights of citizens, and it provided a structure for citizens to be involved in the decisions that affected their lives.

The ancient Greek city-states of Athens and Sparta were the first to have democracy, with citizens voting in assemblies and electing representatives to the council. This system of government established a basis for the development of the modern democratic system seen in the world today.

The Greeks believed in the right of citizens to have a say in the decisions that affected their lives. This belief in equality and justice was reflected in their written laws. It was also evident in their constitution, which provided a framework for the citizens to have a say in the decisions of the government.

The ancient Greeks also developed the concept of citizen participation in the decision-making process. This concept was based on the idea that all citizens should have a say in the decisions that affected their lives. This concept was further developed by the ancient Athenians and incorporated into their democracy.

The ancient Greeks believed that all citizens had the right to be heard and that their opinions should be taken seriously. This belief in the power of citizens to influence the government was reflected in the establishment of the assembly, a system of public meetings where citizens could voice their opinions and take part in the decision-making process. This system of government was the basis for modern democracies.

Greece is still considered the birthplace of democracy and its influence can still be seen in the modern systems of government around the world. The ancient Greeks laid the groundwork for the development of democracy and their legacy still lives on. Greece is a nation with a rich history and culture that still influences the world today. Its democratic system of government was an important part of its history and still shapes the way we think about democracy today.

Greece is widely regarded as the birthplace of democracy, and the ancient Greeks made many lasting contributions to Western civilization in areas such as philosophy, art, science, and politics. The Greek empire spanned over several centuries, with the most influential period being the Classical Age, which lasted from around 500 BC to 323 BC.

The ancient Greeks established city-states, such as Athens and Sparta, which were each governed by their own unique political systems. Athens is particularly known for being the birthplace of democracy, with the creation of the Athenian democracy in the 5th century BC. Athenian democracy was unique in that it allowed citizens to participate in the decision-making process through the use of the Assembly and the Council of 500, both of which were open to all male citizens.

The Greeks were also known for their advancements in philosophy, with philosophers such as Socrates, Plato, and Aristotle making significant contributions to the field. Socrates is known for his method of questioning, which helped to develop the concept of logic and critical thinking. Plato's works, such as The Republic, helped to establish the foundation for political theory, while Aristotle's contributions to science and philosophy helped to shape the way that people thought about the natural world.

Greek art and architecture also had a lasting impact on Western civilization. The Greeks were known for their use of proportion and symmetry, which can be seen in their buildings and sculptures. The Parthenon, a temple dedicated to the goddess Athena, is considered one of the greatest achievements of Greek architecture, while Greek sculpture, such as the Venus de Milo, is considered some of the finest in the world.

The Greeks also made significant contributions to science and medicine, with figures such as Hippocrates, who is considered the father of modern medicine, and Pythagoras, who is known for his contributions to mathematics.

While the Greek empire eventually declined and was conquered by the Romans in the 2nd century BC, its legacy has endured. Greek ideas and traditions have continued to influence Western civilization, from the creation of modern democracy to the development of philosophy, art, and science. Today, Greece remains a cultural and historical hub, with many of its ancient ruins and monuments still standing as a testament to the enduring legacy of this remarkable civilization.

ROME: FROM REPUBLIC TO EMPIRE

The history of Rome is one of the most complex and fascinating stories of any civilization. Its journey from a small city-state to the dominant force in the Mediterranean and beyond is a remarkable tale of power, ambition and success.

The Roman Republic began in 509 BCE with the overthrow of the Etruscan king. The republic was founded on the principles of shared power between the Senate and the people, and it was a time of great progress and prosperity. Rome was able to expand its territories, defeating rival powers and establishing control over vast swathes of the Mediterranean. It was during this period that Rome became the center of the Mediterranean world and a major power.

The Republic eventually succumbed to civil war, and Julius Caesar emerged as the victor. Caesar was assassinated in 44 BCE, and his grand-nephew Octavian emerged as the new leader. Octavian was later declared Augustus, the first Emperor of Rome. Under Augustus, the Roman Empire was established, and Rome flourished as a superpower.

The Roman Empire was one of the most powerful empires in the ancient world and it lasted for over 500 years. The Empire was divided into two parts, the Western and Eastern Roman Empire, which were ruled by separate emperors.

Rome is one of the most iconic empires in history, spanning from the 8th century BC to the 5th century AD. The Roman Republic was established in 509 BC, and was characterized by a system of government in which power was shared between two consuls and a Senate. However, the republic eventually gave way to the Roman Empire, which was marked by the reign of powerful emperors and significant territorial expansion.

The Roman Republic was characterized by a complex system of government and law. In addition to the consuls and Senate, the republic also had a system of magistrates and a popular assembly. The Twelve Tables, a set of laws created in the 5th century BC, formed the basis of Roman law and were instrumental in shaping Western legal systems.

The Roman Republic was also marked by a series of military conquests, which helped to establish Rome as a dominant power in the Mediterranean region. Rome's military success was due in part to its innovative military tactics, such as the use of the phalanx and the creation of a professional army.

In the 1st century BC, Rome entered a period of political instability known as the Roman Civil War. The conflict ultimately resulted in the rise of Julius Caesar, who was appointed dictator for life in 44 BC. However, Caesar was assassinated just one year later, and the Roman Republic was once again plunged into chaos.

In the aftermath of Caesar's death, the Roman Empire was established. The first emperor, Augustus, was appointed in 27 BC, and during his reign, he oversaw significant territorial expansion, including the conquest of Egypt. The empire was characterized by a system of absolute rule, with the emperor holding all political power.

The Roman Empire continued to expand and grow throughout the 1st and 2nd centuries AD, but by the 3rd century, it had begun to experience significant political and economic instability. The empire was ultimately divided into two parts in 395 AD, with the Western Roman Empire falling to invasions by Germanic tribes in the 5th century AD.

Despite its eventual decline, the Roman Empire had a lasting impact on Western civilization. Roman law and government were instrumental in shaping modern political and legal systems, while Roman architecture and engineering, such as the aqueducts and roads, continue to influence modern infrastructure. The Latin language, which was spoken by the Romans, also had a significant impact on the development of European languages.

The transition from republic to empire was a gradual process that occurred over several centuries, marked by political instability, military expansion, and social and economic changes.

The Roman Republic was characterized by a complex system of government that included two consuls, a Senate, and popular assemblies. During the republic era, Rome became a dominant power in the Mediterranean world through a series of military conquests, expansion of its territories and colonization of new lands.

In the 1st century BC, the Roman Republic became embroiled in a series of civil wars that resulted in the collapse of the republican system of government. The Roman general Julius Caesar emerged as a powerful political figure, and after his assassination, his adopted son Octavian (later known as Augustus) became the first Roman emperor.

Augustus reorganized the Roman government and transformed it into an imperial system that was characterized by a single ruler holding absolute power. He established a professional standing army, strengthened the economy, and initiated public works projects to improve infrastructure throughout the empire.

Under Augustus, the Roman Empire continued to expand and consolidate its power, conquering new territories and spreading

Roman culture and values throughout the Mediterranean world. The empire experienced a period of peace and prosperity known as the Pax Romana, which lasted for over two centuries. During this time, the Romans made significant contributions to architecture, engineering, and the arts. They built impressive structures, such as the Colosseum and aqueducts, that still stand as symbols of their power and engineering expertise. Roman art and literature also had a profound impact on Western culture, with notable works including the epic poem "The Aeneid" by Virgil and the histories of Livy.

However, the Roman Empire eventually faced significant challenges, including invasions by barbarian tribes and economic and political instability. By the 5th century AD, the Western Roman Empire had collapsed, and the Eastern Roman Empire, known as the Byzantine Empire, continued to survive until the 15th century.

Despite its eventual decline, the Roman Empire's legacy lives on in many aspects of modern Western civilization. The Roman legal system and principles of governance continue to influence modern political and legal systems, while Roman architecture and engineering have inspired generations of builders and architects. The Latin language, the official language of the Roman Empire, has also had a significant impact on the development of modern European languages.

THE FALL OF ROME

The fall of the Roman Empire is a complex and multi-faceted event that occurred over a period of several centuries. While historians have debated the specific factors that led to the fall, it is generally agreed upon that a combination of internal and external pressures contributed to the decline and eventual collapse of the empire.

One major factor in the fall of Rome was political instability. After the death of the emperor Marcus Aurelius in 180 AD, the empire entered a period of political turmoil and instability known as the Crisis of the Third Century. During this time, Rome was plagued by civil wars, coups, and military mutinies that weakened the government and undermined the authority of the emperor.

Economic factors also played a role in the fall of Rome. The empire faced increasing financial burdens, such as the cost of maintaining its extensive military and infrastructure, while also experiencing a decline in agricultural productivity and trade. This led to inflation and economic instability, which in turn contributed to social unrest and political instability.

External pressures also contributed to the fall of Rome. The empire faced repeated invasions by barbarian tribes, particularly from the north and east. These invasions put a strain on the Roman military, which was already weakened by internal conflicts and financial difficulties.

Despite attempts by emperors to reform and strengthen the empire, the political, economic, and military challenges facing Rome proved too great. In 476 AD, the last Western Roman emperor, Romulus Augustus, was deposed by the Germanic king Odoacer, marking the end of the Western Roman Empire.

However, the Eastern Roman Empire, known as the Byzantine Empire, continued to survive until the 15th century. This empire, which was based in Constantinople (modern-day Istanbul), continued to be a major power in the Mediterranean world for centuries.

The fall of Rome had significant consequences for Western civilization. It marked the end of a period of political and cultural unity and contributed to a period of turmoil and fragmentation in Europe. It also marked the beginning of the Middle Ages, a period characterized by political decentralization and social and economic upheaval. However, the legacy of Rome continued to shape Western civilization in many ways, from its legal and political systems to its architecture and art.

PART II: MEDIEVAL EMPIRES
BYZANTINE EMPIRE: THE EASTERN ROMAN EMPIRE

The Byzantine Empire, often referred to as the Eastern Roman Empire, was a state that existed from 395 to 1453 and was the continuation of the Roman Empire in its eastern provinces. It was centered around the city of Constantinople (modern-day Istanbul), now the capital of Turkey. The Empire was founded by Constantine the Great and was the longest-lasting of the Roman successor states.

The Byzantine Empire was the most powerful and influential state in the Eastern Mediterranean for more than a thousand years and was the largest and wealthiest state in Europe for much of the Middle Ages. At its height, the Byzantine Empire stretched from the southern border of the Danube in the north to Syria and the Holy Land in the south, and from the Black Sea in the east to the Adriatic Sea in the west.

The Byzantines were known for their great achievements in art, architecture, literature, and science. They developed a unique culture, and their religious practices blended Eastern and Western traditions. In addition, the Byzantines made significant advances in military technology, particularly in the use of siege engines and fortifications.

The Byzantine Empire is remembered for its great political and economic stability. It remained the largest and most powerful Christian state for hundreds of years, and its influence spread far beyond its borders. Despite its eventual decline, the legacy of the Byzantine Empire is still felt in the modern world.

The Byzantine Empire is often remembered as the final bastion of the Roman Empire and a crucial link between the Classical and Medieval worlds. Its legacy lives on in the form of the Eastern Orthodox Church, which still claims to be the continuation of the Byzantine Empire. The Byzantine Empire is also credited with preserving many of the Classical Greek and Roman texts, leading to the Renaissance of Europe.

It lasted for over a thousand years, from the founding of Constantinople in 324 CE by the Emperor Constantine until the fall of the city to the Ottoman Turks in 1453 CE.

The Byzantine Empire was known for its rich cultural and artistic heritage, as well as its strong military and political power. Its capital, Constantinople, was one of the most important cities in the world during the medieval period and was a major center of trade, diplomacy, and scholarship.

The Byzantine Empire had a complex political system, with a powerful emperor who was both the head of the state and the head of the Orthodox Church. The emperor ruled over a vast and diverse population that included Greeks, Armenians, Syrians, Egyptians, and other peoples. The empire was also home to a large number of Jews, who were often persecuted but also played an important role in the economy and culture of the empire.

The Byzantine Empire faced many challenges throughout its history, including invasions by barbarian tribes, religious conflicts, and economic crises. The empire also engaged in many wars, both defensive and offensive, and fought against many powerful enemies, including the Persians, the Arabs, and the Bulgars.

Despite these challenges, the Byzantine Empire was able to survive for over a thousand years, thanks to its strong military, effective bureaucracy, and innovative economic policies. It also made significant contributions to the development of art, architecture, literature, philosophy, and science, and played an important role in the spread of Christianity in Europe and the Middle East.

The Byzantine Empire finally came to an end in 1453, when Constantinople was conquered by the Ottoman Turks. However, its legacy lived on in the culture and traditions of the Orthodox Church, as well as in the art and literature of the Renaissance period, which was heavily influenced by Byzantine styles and themes. Today, the Byzantine Empire remains a fascinating and important chapter in the history of Europe and the Mediterranean world.

ISLAMIC CALIPHATE: UNITY AND EXPANSION

The Islamic Caliphate was a medieval empire that emerged in the 7th century CE and quickly spread throughout much of the Middle East, North Africa, and parts of Europe and Asia. It was founded by the Prophet Muhammad, who is considered the last prophet in Islam, and his followers, and was initially centered in the Arabian Peninsula.

The early years of the Islamic Caliphate were marked by rapid expansion and military conquests. Under the first four caliphs, known as the Rashidun Caliphs, the empire grew to encompass much of the Arabian Peninsula, Persia, Iraq, and parts of Syria and Egypt.

One of the key factors in the success of the Islamic Caliphate was its unity and cohesion. Despite the fact that the empire was made up of a diverse array of tribes, ethnic groups, and religious sects, it was able to maintain a strong sense of shared identity and purpose. This was largely due to the unifying power of Islam, which provided a common set of beliefs and values that transcended tribal and ethnic differences.

The Islamic Caliphate also benefited from a highly centralized system of government, with a strong caliph at its head who wielded significant political, military, and religious authority. This allowed the caliphate to respond quickly and decisively to external threats and internal challenges, and to maintain a high level of organizational efficiency.

Another key factor in the success of the Islamic Caliphate was its military prowess. The empire relied on a powerful army of highly skilled and disciplined soldiers, who were trained in the art of warfare and were motivated by a strong sense of loyalty and devotion to Islam. The Islamic Caliphate was able to defeat many powerful enemies, including the Byzantine and Sassanian empires, thanks to its superior military tactics, organization, and strategy.

As the Islamic Caliphate expanded, it also became a center of trade, commerce, and scholarship. The empire was home to many important cities, including Damascus, Baghdad, and Cairo, which served as centers of culture, learning, and innovation. Muslim scholars made significant contributions to fields such as mathematics, astronomy, medicine, and philosophy, and helped to preserve and transmit the knowledge of the ancient Greeks and Romans.

One of the key features of the Islamic Caliphate was its tolerance for other religions and cultures. Although Islam was the dominant religion of the empire, non-Muslims were allowed to practice their own faiths and were often given protection and support by the government. This policy of tolerance helped to promote a spirit of diversity and pluralism within the empire, and helped to foster a sense of mutual respect and understanding among different religious and ethnic groups.

Despite its many achievements, the Islamic Caliphate was not without its challenges and setbacks. The empire faced internal strife and political instability, particularly during the later years of the Abbasid dynasty, which saw a decline in central authority and the rise of regional powers. The empire also faced external threats from the Crusaders, who launched a series of military campaigns to try to recapture the Holy Land from Muslim control.

The Islamic Caliphate finally came to an end in the 13th century, when it was conquered by the Mongol Empire under Genghis Khan and his successors. The Mongol conquest was a devastating blow to the Islamic world, and marked the beginning of a period of political fragmentation and decline.

Despite its eventual collapse, the Islamic Caliphate remains an important and influential chapter in world history. It was a period of great cultural and intellectual achievement, as well as a time of rapid expansion and military conquest. The empire's legacy can be seen in the many contributions it made to science, art, literature, and philosophy, as well as in the enduring impact of Islam on world history and culture.

The Islamic Caliphate Medieval Empire united many different ethnic, cultural, and religious communities under a single rule. The Caliphate was based on Islamic law and Islamic values, and its leaders sought to expand the Islamic faith throughout the empire. The Caliphate was led by the caliph, who was an appointed ruler that had the power to enact laws and administer justice.

The Islamic Caliphate Medieval Empire was an incredibly powerful force that brought about great advances in the fields of science, mathematics, architecture, and the arts. During this period, the Islamic world made significant contributions to the development of philosophy, astronomy, engineering, and medicine. In addition, the Islamic world was a major center of trade and commerce, and was an important political force in the Middle East and North Africa.

The Islamic Caliphate Medieval Empire was a major force in the expansion of Islam and the spread of Islamic culture. Although the empire was eventually destroyed by the Mongol invasions in the 13th century, its impact and legacy still remain in many parts of the world today.

MONGOL EMPIRE: THE CONQUERORS OF THE STEPPES

The Mongol Empire was one of the most successful empires in history and was founded by Genghis Khan in 1206. It stretched from the Pacific Ocean to the Baltic Sea, and from Siberia to the Middle East.

The Mongol Empire was built upon a nomadic lifestyle that enabled them to move quickly and outmaneuver their enemies. They also used psychological warfare to intimidate their opponents and had a very effective military strategy.

The Mongol Empire was known for its fierce warriors and their ability to conquer vast territories. They were particularly successful in their conquest of China and the Middle East, and they were also able to bring much of Central Asia under their control.

The Mongol Empire was considered a great success because of their ability to establish a large and powerful empire in a short period of time. They were able to create a unified nation under the rule of Genghis Khan and his successors, and they were able to maintain control of their territories for many years.

The Mongol Empire is also remembered for its great achievements in the arts and sciences. The empire was home to many renowned scientists, artists, and scholars, and it was during this period that many important scientific and cultural advances were made.

The Mongol Empire was eventually defeated by the Chinese and the Russians, but its legacy lives on in the form of many of the modern nation-states that exist today. The Mongol Empire was an incredible example of how a conquering force can succeed in creating an empire and controlling a vast territory.

The Mongol Empire was an incredible example of the power of the steppes, and the abilities of the nomadic warriors who lived there. The Mongol Empire was one of the most successful empires in history and has left a lasting legacy that we can still learn from today.

The Mongol Empire was one of the largest and most powerful empires in world history, spanning much of Asia and Europe during the 13th and 14th centuries. It was founded by Genghis Khan, a Mongolian warrior and statesman who united the various tribes of the steppes and transformed them into a powerful military force.

Genghis Khan began his conquests in the early 13th century, first consolidating his control over the tribes of Mongolia and then launching a series of devastating campaigns against neighboring kingdoms and empires. His armies swept through China, Central Asia, and Eastern Europe, leaving a trail of destruction and terror in their wake.

One of the keys to the success of the Mongol Empire was its military organization and strategy. Mongol armies were highly disciplined and mobile, able to move quickly across vast distances and engage in surprise attacks against their enemies. They also made use of innovative tactics, such as feigned retreats and false flank attacks, to confuse and defeat their opponents.

Another factor in the success of the Mongol Empire was its system of governance. The Mongols were adept at administering the vast territories they conquered, relying on a decentralized system of local administration and taxation that allowed them to maintain control over diverse populations and cultures. They also established a sophisticated network of trade routes and diplomatic alliances, which helped to sustain the empire's economy and political power.

Despite their reputation as ruthless conquerors, the Mongols were also responsible for significant cultural and intellectual achievements. They patronized the arts and sciences, and made significant contributions to fields such as astronomy, medicine, and literature. They also helped to spread ideas and technologies across Eurasia, contributing to the growth of a vibrant and diverse global civilization.

However, the Mongol Empire was not without its challenges and setbacks. In the late 13th century, internal disputes and political instability led to the fragmentation of the empire, and by the 14th century it had largely disintegrated into a collection of smaller states and territories. The empire also faced external threats, including resistance from local populations and invasions by other empires, such as the Timurids and the Ming Dynasty.

Despite its eventual decline, the Mongol Empire left a lasting impact on world history. Its conquests and cultural achievements helped to shape the political, economic, and cultural landscape of Eurasia, and its legacy can still be seen in the many languages, customs, and traditions of the region today. The Mongol Empire remains a symbol of the power and potential of nomadic societies, and a testament to the enduring human capacity for innovation, resilience, and adaptability.

AZTEC EMPIRE: THE LAND OF THE SUN

The Aztec Empire, also known as the Triple Alliance, was a Mesoamerican civilization that flourished in what is now Central and South America from the 14th to 16th centuries. It was one of the largest empires in the Americas and its capital city, Tenochtitlan, was the largest city in the world when it was founded in 1325. The Aztecs were a highly organized and powerful people who developed a complex culture and society, with a focus on human sacrifice, elaborate religious ceremonies and a powerful military. The Aztec Empire was tributary, meaning that it extracted tribute from its conquered subjects. This tribute was used to finance the Aztecs' public works projects and military campaigns.

The Aztecs were highly religious and believed in a pantheon of gods, with the sun god Huitzilopochtli being the most important. The Aztec people were also known as the "People of the Sun" and believed that their civilization was the chosen one to bring about the fifth sun. They built grand temples and pyramids dedicated to their gods and held grand festivals to celebrate the sun's annual rebirth. The Aztecs were also skilled warriors and developed an impressive arsenal of weapons, including the macuahuitl and the atlatl, which were used to great effect in their conquest of much of Mesoamerica.

The Aztec Empire was eventually defeated by the Spanish in 1521. However, aspects of Aztec culture, such as language and art, remain today in the form of the Nahua people, who are direct descendants of the Aztecs. The Aztec Empire was a powerful force in Mesoamerica and left an indelible mark on the region and the world.

The Aztec Empire, also known as the Triple Alliance, was one of the most powerful and influential empires of pre-Columbian America. It was centered in the Valley of Mexico and flourished during the 14th, 15th, and 16th centuries. The empire was characterized by a complex and highly developed social, economic, and political system, as well as a rich artistic and cultural heritage.

The Aztecs, also known as the Mexica, were a tribe of people who migrated from the north and settled in the Valley of Mexico in the 13th century. They established their capital city, Tenochtitlan, on an island in the middle of Lake Texcoco, and gradually built a powerful empire through a combination of military conquest and diplomatic alliances.

One of the defining features of the Aztec Empire was its social and political organization. At the top of the hierarchy was the emperor, who was regarded as a divine figure and held absolute power over the empire. Below the emperor was a series of nobles, priests, and administrators who helped to govern the empire and oversee its many institutions.

The Aztecs also had a highly developed economic system, based on a combination of agriculture, trade, and tribute. They grew a wide variety of crops, including maize, beans, and squash, and traded extensively with neighboring tribes and empires. They also collected tribute from conquered territories, which helped to fuel the empire's growth and expansion.

Another defining feature of the Aztec Empire was its religion and culture. The Aztecs worshipped a pantheon of gods and goddesses, and their religious practices were highly ritualistic and complex. They also had a rich artistic and literary tradition, including the creation of intricate sculptures, paintings, and manuscripts.

Despite its many achievements, the Aztec Empire was not without its flaws and challenges. The empire's dependence on tribute and conquest led to widespread resistance and rebellion among its subject peoples, and its religious practices and human sacrifices were often viewed with horror by outsiders.

The Aztec Empire also faced a significant external threat in the form of the Spanish conquest. In 1519, the Spanish explorer Hernan Cortes arrived in Mexico and, with the help of native allies, gradually overthrew the Aztec Empire. The conquest was marked by intense violence and bloodshed and had a profound impact on the history and culture of Mexico and Latin America. Today, the legacy of the Aztec Empire can be seen in the many cultural, artistic, and linguistic traditions of Mexico and Central America. The empire remains a testament to the ingenuity and resilience of the indigenous peoples of the Americas and a reminder of the rich and diverse history of the region.

INCA EMPIRE: THE LAND OF THE FOUR QUARTERS

The Inca Empire, also known as the Land of the Four Quarters, was a South American empire that flourished in the 15th and 16th centuries. It was centered in modern-day Peru and is considered one of the greatest civilizations in pre-Columbian America. The Inca Empire was divided into four quarters, each ruled by an emperor or king. These four quarters were the north, south, east, and west, and were considered the four corners of the world.

The Inca Empire was highly organized and elaborate, with an advanced economy and a strong military. The Inca were skilled farmers and engineers, and they built an extensive network of roads and bridges to connect the four quarters. They also developed an advanced system of taxation and trade, and their political and religious structure was highly organized.

The Inca Empire was remarkable for its incredible achievements in architecture, art, engineering, and mathematics. They are particularly known for their monumental stone structures, such as Machu Picchu and the Temple of the Sun. The Inca Empire was also known for its impressive textile craftsmanship and metalwork.

The Inca Empire was conquered by the Spanish in the 16th century, but its legacy lives on today. The Inca people are still present in Peru and continue to practice the traditional customs and beliefs of their ancestors. The Inca Empire remains an inspiration for many, and its legacy continues to be felt today. The Inca Empire, also known as Tawantinsuyu, was the largest and most powerful empire in pre-Columbian America. It was centered in the Andean region of South America and encompassed a vast territory that spanned modern-day Peru, Bolivia, Ecuador, Chile, and Argentina. The empire was characterized by a sophisticated social, economic, and political system, as well as a rich artistic and cultural heritage.

The Inca Empire was founded by the legendary ruler Manco Capac in the early 13th century. Over the next several centuries, the empire expanded through a combination of military conquest and strategic alliances, eventually becoming one of the largest and most advanced empires in the world.

One of the defining features of the Inca Empire was its social and political organization. At the top of the hierarchy was the Inca, who was regarded as divine figure and held absolute power over the empire. Below the Inca were a series of nobles, priests, and administrators who helped to govern the empire and oversee its many institutions.

The Inca Empire also had a highly developed economic system, based on a combination of agriculture, trade, and tribute. They were known for their advanced agricultural techniques, such as terrace farming and irrigation systems, which allowed them to grow a wide variety of crops in the Andean highlands. They also had an extensive network of roads and bridges that facilitated trade and communication throughout the empire.

Another defining feature of the Inca Empire was its religion and culture. The Incas worshipped a pantheon of gods and goddesses, and their religious practices were highly ritualistic and complex. They also had a rich artistic and literary tradition, including the creation of intricate textiles, pottery, and metalwork.

Despite its many achievements, the Inca Empire was not without its flaws and challenges. The empire's rapid expansion and centralized control led to widespread resistance and rebellion among its subject peoples, and its religious practices and human sacrifices were often viewed with horror by outsiders.

The Inca Empire also faced a significant external threat in the form of the Spanish conquest. In 1532, the Spanish explorer Francisco Pizarro arrived in Peru and, with the help of native allies, gradually overthrew the Inca Empire. The conquest was marked by intense violence and bloodshed and had a profound impact on the history and culture of South America.

Today, the legacy of the Inca Empire can be seen in the many cultural, artistic, and linguistic traditions of Peru and the Andean region. The empire remains a testament to the ingenuity and resilience of the indigenous peoples of the Americas and a reminder of the rich and diverse history of the region.

PART III: EARLY MODERN EMPIRES
SPANISH EMPIRE: THE CONQUISTADORS AND THE NEW WORLD

The Spanish Empire was one of the largest empires in history. Spanning over four centuries and five continents, it was the first global empire to exist. At its peak, its population was estimated to have been as high as 17 million people.

The Spanish Empire began in 1492 when Christopher Columbus arrived in the New World. The Spanish Conquistadors followed Columbus, led by Hernán Cortés who conquered the Aztecs in 1521. The Spanish used their superior weapons and tactics to quickly gain control of much of Central and South America.

In the 16th century, the Spanish Empire continued to expand, taking control of the Caribbean, Florida, and parts of the US Southwest. They imposed their religion, culture, and language on the native peoples they encountered. The Spanish also established a rich colonial culture, introducing new crops such as sugarcane, coffee, and tobacco, as well as many other new products.

The Spanish Empire was not only an economic force but also a military one. They fought wars in Europe, the Caribbean, and the New World. They also built a navy that was unmatched in size and power by any other nation. In the 18th century, the Spanish Empire was weakened by wars and internal conflicts, leading to its eventual decline.

The Spanish Empire left a lasting legacy in the New World. Their language and culture are still present in many parts of the

Americas. In addition, the Spanish were responsible for introducing many new crops and products to the New World, which had a lasting impact on the economy and culture of the Americas.

The Spanish Empire was one of the most powerful and influential empires in history. Its legacy still lives on today in the Americas, serving as a reminder of the great power and influence the Spanish had over the New World.

The Spanish Empire was one of the most powerful empires in world history, stretching across much of the globe at its height in the 16th and 17th centuries. One of the defining aspects of the Spanish Empire was its conquest of the New World, a vast and previously unknown landmass that would become the site of some of the most important events in world history.

The conquest of the New World began in 1492 when Christopher Columbus, an Italian explorer sailing under the flag of the Spanish crown, made landfall in the Bahamas. Over the next several decades, Spanish explorers known as Conquistadors would venture further into the New World, establishing colonies and subjugating the indigenous peoples they encountered.

Perhaps the most famous of the Conquistadors was Hernán Cortés, who in 1519 led an expedition that would ultimately lead to the fall of the Aztec Empire. Cortés and his men were aided by internal divisions within the Aztec Empire, as well as the belief among the indigenous people that Cortés was a god or a powerful supernatural being.

Other notable Conquistadors include Francisco Pizarro, who conquered the Inca Empire in what is now Peru, and Juan Ponce de León, who is credited with the discovery of Florida. These men and others like them were driven by a desire for wealth, power, and glory, and were willing to do whatever it took to achieve their goals.

The conquest of the New World was not without its controversies and atrocities. The Spanish Conquistadors often used brutal tactics to subjugate the indigenous peoples they encountered, including slavery, forced conversion to Christianity, and outright genocide. Millions of indigenous people died as a result of disease, warfare, and forced labor under the Spanish colonial system.

Despite these dark aspects of the conquest, the Spanish Empire left an indelible mark on the New World. Spanish language and culture remain influential in many parts of Latin America, and Spanish colonization helped to shape the political, economic, and social structures of many modern-day countries in the region.

In conclusion, the Spanish Empire and its Conquistadors played a significant role in the conquest of the New World, leaving a lasting impact on the history and culture of the region. While the actions of the Conquistadors were often brutal and oppressive, their legacy cannot be ignored or forgotten.

PORTUGUESE EMPIRE: THE AGE OF EXPLORATION

The Portuguese Empire was a remarkable period of exploration and expansion that took place from the 15th to the 19th century.

It was during this time that Portugal established a vast network of colonies, trading posts, and forts that stretched from the coast of Africa to India and beyond. The Portuguese Empire was, in many ways, the first truly global empire, and its success was due in large part to the Age of Exploration.

The Age of Exploration was a period in which European nations began to explore and expand their holdings in regions outside of Europe. Portugal was one of the leaders in this endeavor, and its sailors were some of the most successful navigators and explorers of the time. These explorers set out to discover new lands and resources, and to expand Portugal's influence in the world.

The Portuguese exploration of the world was largely driven by their desire to find a sea route to India. This search ultimately led them to Africa, where they established several trading posts and eventually even built a small empire. From these bases, Portuguese explorers were able to explore much of the African coastline and even venture into the Indian Ocean. From there, they were able to establish trading posts in India, the Spice Islands, and other parts of Asia.

The Portuguese Empire was one of the great European empires of the 15th and 16th centuries. It was built on the foundation of the Age of Exploration, a period of maritime expansion and colonization that began in the 15th century and continued until the early 17th century. Portuguese explorers played a pivotal role in this era, opening up new trade routes, establishing colonies, and building a global network of commerce.

The Portuguese Age of Exploration began in the early 15th century with the voyages of Prince Henry the Navigator, who established a school of navigation and exploration in Sagres, Portugal. His expeditions along the West African coast paved the way for future explorers, such as Vasco da Gama, who in 1498 sailed around the southern tip of Africa and reached India, opening up a new trade route to the East.

The Portuguese also played a major role in the colonization of the Americas, establishing settlements in Brazil and making contact with indigenous peoples throughout the continent. However, unlike the Spanish, who conquered and subjugated indigenous populations, the Portuguese focused primarily on trade and commerce, establishing trading posts and building alliances with local rulers.

One of the key aspects of the Portuguese Empire was its focus on maritime trade, which was facilitated by the development of new navigational technologies such as the astrolabe and the caravel. The Portuguese also played a major role in the development of the slave trade, which was a major source of labor for European colonies in the Americas and elsewhere.

Despite its many achievements, the Portuguese Empire was not without its controversies and failures. The empire suffered from internal political and economic struggles, and its attempts to establish colonies in Africa and Asia often led to violent conflict with local populations. Additionally, the Portuguese were eventually eclipsed by other European powers such as the Spanish, Dutch, and British, who established their global empires and challenged Portuguese dominance in trade and commerce.

In conclusion, the Portuguese Empire played a crucial role in the Age of Exploration, opening up new trade routes, establishing colonies, and building a global network of commerce. Its legacy can be seen in the many countries around the world where the Portuguese language and culture remain influential, as well as in the lasting impact of Portuguese colonization on the history and development of many regions of the world.

OTTOMAN EMPIRE: THE RISE AND DECLINE OF A MUSLIM POWER

The Ottoman Empire was a Muslim power that rose to prominence during the 13th century and lasted until its dissolution in the early 20th century. It was one of the longest-lasting Muslim empires and its influence stretched from the Mediterranean to the Caucasus, North Africa, and the Balkans. The Ottoman Empire began as a small principality in Anatolia (modern-day Turkey) in 1299, under the rule of Osman I. The Ottoman dynasty quickly expanded into the surrounding region, conquering the Byzantine Empire in 1453 and the Mamluks in 1517. The Ottoman Empire reached its peak in the 16th and 17th centuries when it controlled much of the Middle East, North Africa, and the Balkans.

The Ottoman Empire was a major political and military power in Europe and Asia. It was a powerful economic force, controlling much of the trade in the region. The empire maintained an advanced legal system, a strong bureaucracy, and a flourishing culture. It was also a major center of Islamic learning, producing numerous scholars and jurists.

The decline of the Ottoman Empire began in the early 19th century due to a combination of internal and external pressures. The empire was deeply affected by the French Revolution and the Napoleonic Wars. In addition, the Ottoman government was unable to keep pace with the rise of nationalist movements in the Balkans and elsewhere. The empire was also affected by the industrial revolution and the rise of the European powers.

The Ottoman Empire officially ended in 1923, when the Republic of Turkey was declared. However, the legacy of the Ottoman Empire remains today in the form of Turkish cuisine, language, and culture. The influence of the Ottoman Empire can also be seen in the Middle East, North Africa, and the Balkans.

The Ottoman Empire was a vast, multi-ethnic empire that existed for over six centuries, from its rise in the late 13th century to its dissolution at the end of World War I. It was founded by Osman Bey, a Turkish chieftain who established a small state in the region of Bursa in northwestern Anatolia. Over several centuries, the Ottomans expanded their territory and established themselves as a major power in the Islamic world. They conquered the Byzantine Empire and captured Constantinople, which they renamed Istanbul, in 1453. They also expanded into southeastern Europe, northern Africa, and the Middle East, establishing a vast and diverse empire that was home to numerous ethnic and religious groups.

The Ottomans were renowned for their military prowess, which was based on the use of Janissaries, elite soldiers who were recruited from among the empire's Christian subjects and converted to Islam. They also developed an advanced administrative system that allowed them to govern their vast territories efficiently.

Under the rule of Sultan Suleiman the Magnificent in the 16th century, the Ottoman Empire reached its height of power and prosperity. However, by the 18th century, the empire began to decline, as its military and economic power waned and it faced increasing pressure from European powers.

The Ottomans were eventually drawn into World War I on the side of Germany and Austria-Hungary, but they suffered a series of devastating defeats and were forced to sign the Treaty of Sèvres in 1920, which effectively dissolved the empire. The modern state of Turkey was established soon after, under the leadership of Mustafa Kemal Atatürk, who sought to create a secular, Westernized state.

Despite its decline and dissolution, the Ottoman Empire remains a significant historical and cultural legacy, with enduring influence in the Muslim world and beyond. Its impact on the development of Islamic art, architecture, and culture is still visible today, and its legacy continues to shape the political and social landscape of the Middle East and beyond.

MUGHAL EMPIRE: THE SPLENDOR OF INDIA

The Mughal Empire is one of the most iconic and influential empires to have ever existed in the history of India. The

Mughals ruled India and parts of Afghanistan, Pakistan, and Bangladesh between the 16th and 19th centuries. During this period, the Mughals brought a period of great prosperity and splendor to India, leaving behind a rich cultural legacy that is still celebrated in India today.

The Mughal Empire was founded in 1526 by the Central Asian ruler Babur. He was succeeded by his son Humayun and then by the great Mughal Emperor Akbar. Akbar is widely considered to be the greatest of the Mughal Emperors, and he is credited with elevating the Mughal Empire to its greatest heights. Akbar was a visionary ruler and a great conqueror, and he was responsible for expanding the Mughal Empire to its largest extent.

Under Akbar, the Mughal Empire enjoyed a period of great splendor and grandeur. He was a great patron of the arts and a great builder, and he left behind some of India's most iconic monuments, such as the Taj Mahal, the Red Fort, and the Agra Fort. He also laid the foundations for a centralized, imperial government, and under his rule, the Mughal Empire was a powerful and influential force in India and beyond.

The Mughal Empire left behind a rich legacy in India, including a vibrant and diverse culture, beautiful and sophisticated art and architecture, and vibrant literature. The Mughal Empire also saw the spread of Islam into India and the development of a vibrant new syncretic culture that combined elements of Hinduism, Islam, and other faiths.

The Mughal Empire was eventually dissolved in 1857, but its legacy lives on in India today. The Mughals left behind a rich cultural and architectural heritage that is still celebrated in India, and their legacy has helped shape the culture of India and the subcontinent as a whole.

The Mughal Empire was one of the most powerful and influential empires in India's history, ruling from 1526 to 1857. It was founded by Babur, a descendant of the Mongol conqueror Genghis Khan, who invaded India and defeated the Delhi Sultanate at the Battle of Panipat in 1526.

Under the reign of Babur's grandson, Akbar, the Mughal Empire reached its zenith, becoming one of the wealthiest and most powerful empires in the world. Akbar was a patron of the arts and sciences, and his court was renowned for its splendor and sophistication.

One of Akbar's most significant achievements was his policy of religious tolerance, which allowed Hindus and Muslims to coexist peacefully in his empire. He abolished the jizya tax on non-Muslims and appointed Hindus to high positions in his government, earning him the respect and loyalty of his subjects.

Akbar's successors, Jahangir and Shah Jahan, continued the Mughal tradition of patronizing the arts, and under their rule, the empire reached new heights of cultural and architectural splendor. The Taj Mahal, one of the most iconic buildings in the world, was built by Shah Jahan as a mausoleum for his wife Mumtaz Mahal, and it remains a testament to the Mughal Empire's artistic and architectural achievements.

Despite the Mughals' cultural achievements, the empire faced numerous challenges in the 18th century, as it struggled to maintain control over its vast and diverse territories. The British East India Company gradually gained influence and power, and the Mughals were reduced to figureheads, with the last Mughal emperor, Bahadur Shah Zafar, being exiled to Burma by the British after the Indian Rebellion of 1857.

The legacy of the Mughal Empire is still visible today, both in India and beyond. Its architecture, art, and culture have had a profound influence on Indian society and continue to inspire artists and scholars around the world. The Mughals' policy of religious tolerance and their commitment to cultural and artistic excellence remain enduring legacies, and their contributions to India's rich and diverse heritage continue to be celebrated to this day.

QING EMPIRE: THE LAST OF THE CHINESE DYNASTIES

The Qing Empire was the last of the Chinese dynasties, ruling from 1644 to 1912. It was founded by the Manchus, an ethnic minority from northeastern China. Under their rule, the Qing Empire experienced a period of unprecedented stability and prosperity, becoming the world's largest and most powerful nation.

During the Qing dynasty, the Chinese economy grew rapidly. The government encouraged agricultural production, introduced a new system of taxation, and built extensive transportation networks. Trade also flourished, with many nations trading with China. Moreover, the Qing emperors promoted arts and literature, leading to the flourishing of Chinese culture.

The Qing dynasty also undertook a series of reforms to strengthen its rule. These included the establishment of a centralized bureaucracy, the introduction of a standardized system of laws, and the expansion of the military.

Despite these successes, the Qing dynasty was weakened by internal strife, a series of famines and floods, and the rise of Western imperialism. In the 19th century, the dynasty was increasingly threatened by foreign powers, culminating in the Boxer Rebellion of 1900. Finally, in 1912, the Qing dynasty was overthrown by the forces of the Chinese republican revolution.

The Qing dynasty was the last of the Chinese dynasties, but its legacy is still felt in modern China. Its reforms laid the foundations for the modern Chinese state, while its culture continues to be a source of national pride.

The Qing Empire was the last imperial dynasty in China, ruling from 1644 to 1912. The dynasty was founded by the Manchus, a tribal people from northeast Asia who conquered China and established a new ruling class.

Under the Qing dynasty, China experienced a period of stability and prosperity, as the empire expanded its territory and established itself as a major power in East Asia. The Qing emperors were strong and effective leaders, and they were known for their military prowess, administrative reforms, and patronage of the arts.

One of the most significant achievements of the Qing dynasty was the expansion of China's borders, which reached their greatest extent under the reign of the Qianlong Emperor in the

18th century. The empire also saw significant cultural and artistic developments, particularly in the areas of literature, painting, and calligraphy.

However, the Qing dynasty faced numerous challenges in the 19th century, as it struggled to adapt to the changing political and economic landscape of the world. The empire was weakened by internal rebellion, corruption, and social unrest, as well as by external pressures from European powers, such as the Opium Wars and the Boxer Rebellion.

The downfall of the Qing dynasty came in 1912 when a revolution led by Sun Yat-sen overthrew the imperial government and established the Republic of China. The last emperor, Puyi, was forced to abdicate, marking the end of the 2,000-year-old Chinese imperial system.

Despite its eventual collapse, the Qing Dynasty left a lasting legacy in China and beyond. Its contributions to art, culture, and science continue to be celebrated, and its influence can still be seen in many aspects of Chinese society, from architecture and fashion to language and cuisine. The Qing dynasty remains an important part of China's rich and complex history, and its legacy continues to be studied and debated by scholars and historians around the world.

PART IV: MODERN EMPIRES
BRITISH EMPIRE: THE LARGEST EMPIRE IN HISTORY

The British Empire was the largest in history. Established in the 16th century, it grew to encompass a large portion of the world, including the Americas, India, Australia, Africa, and parts of Asia. At its peak, the British Empire spanned over 13 million square miles and encompassed more than 400 million people. The British Empire was built upon a foundation of trade, exploration, and colonization. British merchants, traders, and explorers traveled to distant lands, establishing trading posts, outposts, and colonies. In addition, the British navy was instrumental in maintaining the empire's dominance in the seas. The British Empire played a pivotal role in the history of the world. It shaped the modern global economy by establishing a trade network that connected distant regions. It also played a key role in the development of democracy and civil rights. The British Empire's influence on language, culture, and education is still felt today.

The British Empire was eventually dismantled in the mid-20th century, after the Second World War. Despite its decline, the legacy of the British Empire remains influential and its impact is still felt in many parts of the world.

The British Empire was the largest and most powerful empire in history, covering a quarter of the world's land area and ruling over a population of approximately 500 million people at its peak. It spanned over 400 years, from the colonization of Ireland in the early 17th century to the gradual decolonization that began after World War II.

The British Empire was founded on the principles of trade, exploration, and colonization. The British established colonies and trading posts throughout the world, from North America to Africa, India, Australia, and the Pacific Islands. The empire was based on a system of exploitation, in which the colonizers benefited from the labor, resources, and markets of the colonized peoples.

The empire was built through a combination of military conquest and diplomatic negotiation. The British fought numerous wars to establish and maintain their control over their colonies, including the Seven Years' War, the Napoleonic Wars, and the Opium Wars. They also used diplomacy to expand their influence, negotiating treaties and alliances with local rulers and governments.

The British Empire brought both benefits and challenges to the colonized peoples. It brought trade and economic development to many regions, as well as the spread of the English language, technology, and cultural values. However, it also brought exploitation, cultural domination, and political subjugation, often resulting in social and economic inequality, displacement, and violence.

The decline of the British Empire began after World War II, as nationalist movements and anti-colonial struggles emerged in many of the colonized regions. The British government responded by granting independence to many of its colonies, beginning with India in 1947. The process of decolonization continued throughout the 20th century, culminating in the handover of Hong Kong to China in 1997.

Despite its eventual decline, the British Empire remains an important part of world history, shaping the political, economic, and cultural landscape of many regions. Its legacy can be seen in the English language, the Commonwealth of Nations, and the enduring influence of British institutions and cultural values. The impact of the British Empire, both positive and negative, continues to be studied and debated by scholars and historians around the world.

FRENCH EMPIRE: FROM REVOLUTION TO COLONIALISM

The French Empire was a powerful force in world affairs for over a century, beginning with the French Revolution of 1789 and ending with the dismantling of the colonial empire following World War II. During this period, France expanded its colonial holdings across the globe, bringing its culture and language to far-flung parts of the world.

Before the Revolution, France was a monarchy, ruled by the Bourbon dynasty. The Revolution saw the overthrow of the monarchy and the establishment of a Republic, as well as the adoption of the Declaration of the Rights of Man and of the Citizen, which declared the equality of all citizens. This new government sought to expand its influence abroad and soon began to acquire colonies in the Caribbean, North America, Africa, and Asia.

The French Empire was a major contributor to the development of many of its colonies. The French introduced a variety of advances in technology, education, and administration to its colonies, which helped to strengthen the colonies' economies and improve their living standards. The French also established a variety of cultural and educational institutions throughout their colonies, which helped to spread the French language and culture to the wider world.

The French Empire was weakened following the disastrous Napoleonic Wars, which saw the loss of much of the colonial empire. The Second French Empire, established in 1852, sought to restore French power and influence but ultimately failed. Following the end of World War II, the French Empire was dismantled and its colonies were granted independence. In the aftermath of the war, France and its former colonies developed new economic and political ties, as well as cultural and educational exchanges.

Today, the legacy of the French Empire can still be seen in many countries around the world. The French language is still spoken in some of the former colonies, and many countries still have French-influenced cultures, architecture, and cuisine. The impact of French imperialism is still felt today, and its legacy will continue to be a major part of the world's history for many years to come.

The French Empire was a colonial empire that existed from the late 16th century to the mid-20th century. It was founded during the era of exploration and colonization and was shaped by the political and cultural developments of the French Revolution. The French Revolution of 1789 led to the rise of Napoleon Bonaparte, who became the emperor of France in 1804. Under his rule, France expanded its empire through military conquest, including the annexation of Belgium, the Netherlands, and parts of Italy, Germany, and Spain. Napoleon also established colonies in the Caribbean, Africa, and Southeast Asia.

After Napoleon's defeat in 1815, France experienced a period of instability and political upheaval, but it continued to expand its colonial empire. France established colonies in Algeria, Indochina, and West Africa, among other places, and became a major player in the "Scramble for Africa," the European race to colonize the continent.

France's colonial empire brought both benefits and challenges to the colonized peoples. On the one hand, it brought economic development and cultural exchange, as well as the spread of the French language and culture. On the other hand, it also brought exploitation, cultural domination, and political subjugation, resulting in social and economic inequality, violence, and displacement.

The French Empire faced numerous challenges in the 20th century, including World War I, and World War II, and the rise of nationalist and anti-colonial movements in its colonies. France granted independence to many of its colonies in the 1950s and 1960s, although it maintained some overseas territories and protectorates.

Today, the legacy of the French Empire can be seen in the French language, culture, and institutions, as well as in the ongoing debates about its impact on the colonized peoples. The French Empire remains an important part of world history, shaping the political, economic, and cultural landscape of many regions, and its legacy continues to be studied and debated by scholars and historians around the world.

RUSSIAN EMPIRE: THE TSARS AND THE EXPANSION EASTWARDS

The Russian Empire was an expansive empire that spanned from Europe to Asia. It was founded in 1721 by Tsar Peter the Great, but it was not until the reign of Tsar Alexander I that the empire started to expand eastwards. During this period, the Tsars sought to increase the power of the Russian Empire by expanding its borders into Central Asia and Siberia.

The process of expansion began with the conquering of the Khanates of the Caucasus, located in present-day Georgia, Armenia, and Azerbaijan. This was followed by the annexation of Crimea in 1783 and the conquest of the Khanate of Bukhara in 1868. By the end of the 19th century, the Russian Empire had come to control most of Central Asia, including the Khanates of Khiva, Bukhara, and Kokand.

In addition to its territorial gains, the Russian Empire also sought to exert its influence over its newly acquired territories in the form of Orthodox Christianity, the Russian language, and the Russian state structure. This process of Russification was embraced by many of the local peoples, who found that the

Russian Empire offered them a higher standard of living than what they were accustomed to.

In the late 19th century, the Tsars also sought to extend their rule into East Asia, beginning with the acquisition of the Amur region in 1858. This was followed by the annexation of the Chinese port of Port Arthur in 1898 and the acquisition of Sakhalin Island in 1905. By the early 20th century, the Russian Empire had become the largest and most powerful nation in the world.

Despite its success, the Russian Empire ultimately fell apart in 1917 due to the Bolshevik Revolution. The Tsars and their expansionist policies had caused much internal strife, and the autocratic rule of the Tsars alienated the people and weakened the Tsar's rule. Nevertheless, the legacy of the Russian Empire remains in the form of its vast borders, which still exist today. The Russian Empire was a multiethnic state that existed from 1721 until 1917 when it was overthrown by the Bolshevik Revolution. The empire was ruled by a series of tsars, or emperors, who oversaw a vast territory that covered one-sixth of the world's land area and included a diverse range of cultures and peoples.

The Russian Empire was founded by Peter the Great, who modernized and expanded the country during his reign from 1682 to 1725. Under Peter's rule, Russia became a major European power, and he sought to "westernize" the country by adopting European customs and technologies.

The Russian Empire continued to expand under subsequent tsars, particularly toward the east. Russian explorers and settlers began to colonize Siberia in the 16th and 17th centuries, and the region became an important source of resources, including furs, minerals, and timber. In the 19th century, Russia expanded into Central Asia, annexing territories such as Kazakhstan, Uzbekistan, and Turkmenistan.

The expansion of the Russian Empire brought both benefits and challenges to the colonized peoples. On the one hand, it brought economic development and cultural exchange, as well as the spread of the Russian language and culture. On the other hand, it also brought exploitation, cultural domination, and political subjugation, resulting in social and economic inequality, violence, and displacement.

The Russian Empire faced numerous challenges in the 20th century, including World War I, the Russian Revolution, and the subsequent Civil War. In 1917, the Bolsheviks overthrew the Tsarist government and established the Soviet Union, which would go on to become a major world power.

Today, the legacy of the Russian Empire can be seen in the Russian language, culture, and institutions, as well as in the ongoing debates about its impact on the colonized peoples. The Russian Empire remains an important part of world history, shaping the political, economic, and cultural landscape of many regions, and its legacy continues to be studied and debated by scholars and historians around the world.

The Russian Empire was an expansive empire that spanned from Europe to Asia. It was founded in 1721 by Tsar Peter the Great, but it was not until the reign of Tsar Alexander I that the empire started to expand eastwards. During this period, the Tsars sought to increase the power of the Russian Empire by expanding its borders into Central Asia and Siberia.

The process of expansion began with the conquering of the Khanates of the Caucasus, located in present-day Georgia, Armenia, and Azerbaijan. This was followed by the annexation of Crimea in 1783 and the conquest of the Khanate of Bukhara in 1868. By the end of the 19th century, the Russian Empire had come to control most of Central Asia, including the Khanates of Khiva, Bukhara, and Kokand.

In addition to its territorial gains, the Russian Empire also sought to exert its influence over its newly acquired territories in the form of Orthodox Christianity, the Russian language, and the Russian state structure. This process of Russification was embraced by many of the local peoples, who found that the Russian Empire offered them a higher standard of living than what they were accustomed to.

In the late 19th century, the Tsars also sought to extend their rule into East Asia, beginning with the acquisition of the Amur region in 1858. This was followed by the annexation of the Chinese port of Port Arthur in 1898 and the acquisition of Sakhalin Island in 1905. By the early 20th century, the Russian Empire had become the largest and most powerful nation in the world.

Despite its success, the Russian Empire ultimately fell apart in 1917 due to the Bolshevik Revolution. The Tsars and their expansionist policies had caused much internal strife, and the autocratic rule of the Tsars alienated the people and weakened the Tsar's rule. Nevertheless, the legacy of the Russian Empire remains in the form of its vast borders, which still exist today. The Russian Empire was a multiethnic state that existed from 1721 until 1917 when it was overthrown by the Bolshevik Revolution. The empire was ruled by a series of tsars, or emperors, who oversaw a vast territory that covered one-sixth of the world's land area and included a diverse range of cultures and peoples.

The Russian Empire was founded by Peter the Great, who modernized and expanded the country during his reign from 1682 to 1725. Under Peter's rule, Russia became a major European power, and he sought to "westernize" the country by adopting European customs and technologies.

The Russian Empire continued to expand under subsequent tsars, particularly toward the east. Russian explorers and settlers began to colonize Siberia in the 16th and 17th centuries, and the region became an important source of resources, including furs, minerals, and timber. In the 19th century, Russia expanded into Central Asia, annexing territories such as Kazakhstan, Uzbekistan, and Turkmenistan.

The expansion of the Russian Empire brought both benefits and challenges to the colonized peoples. On the one hand, it brought economic development and cultural exchange, as well as the spread of the Russian language and culture. On the other hand, it also brought exploitation, cultural domination, and political subjugation, resulting in social and economic inequality, violence, and displacement.

The Russian Empire faced numerous challenges in the 20th century, including World War I, the Russian Revolution, and the subsequent Civil War. In 1917, the Bolsheviks overthrew the Tsarist government and established the Soviet Union, which would go on to become a major world power.

Today, the legacy of the Russian Empire can be seen in the Russian language, culture, and institutions, as well as in the ongoing debates about its impact on the colonized peoples. The Russian Empire remains an important part of world history, shaping the political, economic, and cultural landscape of many regions, and its legacy continues to be studied and debated by scholars and historians around the world.

AMERICAN EMPIRE: THE RISE OF A SUPERPOWER

The American Empire is a term used to describe the United States of America's emergence as a superpower in the late 19th and early 20th centuries. The term is used to describe the country's economic and military power, as well as its cultural and ideological influence.

The rise of the American Empire began with the country's founding in 1776 and the subsequent establishment of a constitutional form of government. From the beginning, the country was marked by its expansive spirit and its belief in the

American Dream of a democratic society and a free-market economy. This spirit, combined with the country's natural resources, enabled the United States to become a powerful economic and political force in the world.

The late 19th and early 20th centuries saw the country become increasingly involved in world affairs. The United States fought in two world wars, which greatly increased its influence and power in the international arena. The country also became involved in numerous foreign interventions, such as the Spanish-American War, World War I, and World War II. These interventions helped to expand the country's military power and influence.

The economic power of the United States also increased during this period. The country experienced rapid economic growth and development, which helped to create a powerful and wealthy nation. This wealth allowed the United States to invest in a variety of international projects, such as the United Nations, the Marshall Plan, and the North Atlantic Treaty Organization.

The American Empire has experienced a period of decline in recent years, as other countries have become more influential in the international arena. Despite this, the United States remains a powerful economic and military superpower and is still a major player in world affairs. The country's influence continues to be felt around the globe, and its commitment to freedom, democracy, and the rule of law remains strong. The United States is likely to remain a superpower for many years to come.

The American Empire is a term used to describe the global influence and power of the United States, particularly since the end of World War II. As the world's largest economy and military power, the United States has played a significant role in shaping global politics, economics, and culture.

The rise of the American Empire began in the late 19th century when the United States began to expand its territory beyond its continental borders. The Spanish-American War of 1898 resulted in the acquisition of Puerto Rico, Guam, and the Philippines, while Hawaii was annexed in 1898.

During World War I, the United States emerged as a major economic and military power, and it played a key role in the defeat of Germany and the other Central Powers. Following the war, the United States became a leading proponent of free trade and international cooperation, and it played a key role in the establishment of the League of Nations.

However, the United States remained largely isolationist in the interwar period, and it did not become fully involved in global affairs until World War II. Following the Japanese attack on Pearl Harbor in 1941, the United States entered the war, and it played a critical role in the Allied victory.

After World War II, the United States emerged as the dominant economic and military power in the world. It played a leading role in the establishment of the United Nations, the World Bank, and the International Monetary Fund, and it also led the fight against Soviet communism during the Cold War.

The American Empire faced numerous challenges in the latter half of the 20th century, including the Vietnam War, the civil rights movement, and the growing influence of anti-American sentiment in many parts of the world. However, the United States remained a global superpower, and it continued to play a leading role in shaping global politics and economics.

Today, the American Empire remains a controversial and divisive topic, with many arguing that the United States should focus more on domestic issues and less on international affairs. However, there is no denying the impact that the American Empire has had on the world, shaping the political, economic, and cultural landscape of many regions, and its legacy continues to be studied and debated by scholars and historians around the world.

JAPANESE EMPIRE: FROM ISOLATION TO EXPANSION

The Japanese Empire was a major power in the early 20th century, stretching from the Russian Far East to China and Southeast Asia. It was an expansionist state that sought to expand its power and influence in the region, and beyond. Its expansion was marked by a period of rapid industrialization and militarization, as well as a series of wars with its neighbors.

For centuries, Japan had been an isolated nation, cut off from much of the world by its insular culture and geography. The Meiji Restoration in the late 19th century saw the country break out of its isolation and begin to modernize, adopting several Western practices and technologies. This modernization, along with a strong sense of national identity and unity, helped the Empire expand its influence and power.

In the early 20th century, the Japanese Empire sought to expand its influence and control in the Asian region. It invaded Korea in 1910 and China in 1931, taking control of some areas. It also became involved in many wars with its neighbors, including the Russo-Japanese War and the Second Sino-Japanese War. These wars saw the Empire gain control of much of Manchuria and large parts of China.

The Japanese Empire was eventually defeated in World War II, after which the country was occupied by the Allies, and its imperialistic ambitions were curtailed. The occupation period saw the establishment of a democratic government and the adoption of a pacifist constitution. Today, Japan is a peaceful and prosperous nation, and its imperial past is largely forgotten.

The Japanese Empire, also known as the Empire of Japan, was a constitutional monarchy that existed from 1868 to 1947. During this period, Japan underwent a dramatic transformation from a feudal society to a modern, industrialized nation, and it emerged as a major player on the world stage.

Before the Meiji Restoration of 1868, Japan had been a largely isolated society, with limited contact with the outside world. However, after the restoration, Japan embarked on a program of modernization and Westernization, adopting many of the political, economic, and cultural practices of Europe and the United States.

As Japan modernized, it began to expand its territory and influence beyond its borders. In 1895, Japan defeated China in the First Sino-Japanese War, gaining control of Taiwan and other territories. In 1905, Japan defeated Russia in the Russo-Japanese War, becoming the first non-Western nation to defeat a major European power.

During World War I, Japan fought on the side of the Allied Powers, and it played a significant role in the war effort, particularly in the Pacific Theater. However, Japan's relationship with the Western powers became strained in the interwar period, particularly after it invaded China in 1937.

In 1941, Japan launched a surprise attack on the United States naval base at Pearl Harbor, Hawaii, bringing the United States into World War II. Japan's aggressive expansionism during the war eventually led to its defeat, and in 1945, the country was occupied by Allied forces.

After the war, Japan underwent a period of reconstruction and modernization, and it emerged as a major economic power in the latter half of the 20th century. Today, Japan is a leading global economy and a major player in international affairs.

The legacy of the Japanese Empire is complex, and it continues to be a subject of debate and controversy. While Japan's modernization and expansion brought many benefits, including economic growth and cultural exchange, it also brought violence, imperialism, and exploitation, particularly in its treatment of its colonies and conquered territories. Today, the Japanese Empire remains an important part of world history, shaping the political, economic, and cultural landscape of many regions, and its legacy continues to be studied and debated by scholars and historians around the world.

CONCLUSION

Throughout human history, empires have risen and fallen, each leaving its mark on the world and shaping the course of history. From the mighty Roman Empire to the British Empire, each empire has had its unique characteristics and impact on global affairs.

Empires rise through a combination of military conquest, political power, and economic influence, but they also fall due to internal decay, external pressures, and shifting geopolitical realities. The rise and fall of empires have been a cyclical pattern throughout human history, with each era marked by the emergence of new powers and the decline of old ones.

Despite their differences, empires share many commonalities, including the pursuit of power and wealth, the exploitation of resources and people, and the imposition of cultural values and norms on conquered territories. While empires have brought about many positive developments, including technological innovations, cultural exchange, and economic growth, they have also caused immense suffering, including wars, oppression, and the loss of cultural identity.

As we reflect on the history of empires, it is important to recognize both their achievements and their shortcomings. By studying the rise and fall of empires, we can gain a deeper understanding of the complexities of human history and the challenges facing us today. As we navigate an increasingly interconnected and rapidly changing world, the lessons of history can provide valuable insights into how we can build a more just and equitable future.

In conclusion, the rise and fall of empires throughout human history have played a major role in shaping the world as we know it today. Empires have come and gone, leaving behind a lasting legacy and a reminder of the power of human ambition, warfare, and the capriciousness of fate. While the reasons behind the rise and fall of empires are varied and complex, the overriding theme is one of the humans living out their destinies and creating lasting legacies as they do so.

The events of human history, be they grand or small, have shaped the world we live in today. Empires have been the backdrop for some of the most significant events in human history, and the lessons to be learned from their rise and fall remain ever-relevant. The rise and fall of empires is a journey through the course of human history, and its study is essential to understanding our past, present, and future.